PLAY BOOK! 2

Baseball

YOU ...are the manager
...call the shots

Tim Cockey

A Sports Illustrated For Kids Book

First Edition

Library of Congress Cataloging-in-Publication Data

Cockey, Tim.
  Playbook! Baseball #2 : you are the manager, you call the shots /
  Tim Cockey. — 1st ed.
      p.   cm.
    "A Sports illustrated for kids book."
    Summary: The reader as team manager makes decisions in this baseball game and then flips pages to see the outcome.
    ISBN 0-316-14923-3
    1. Baseball—Miscellanea—Juvenile literature. 2. Baseball—
Managers—Miscellanea—Juvenile literature.   [1. Baseball—
Miscellanea.   2. Baseball—Managers—Miscellanea.]   I. Title.
II. Title: Baseball number two.
GV867.5.c63   1991
796.357—dc20   90-46196

SPORTS ILLUSTRATED FOR KIDS is a trademark of
THE TIME INC. MAGAZINE COMPANY.

Sports Illustrated For Kids Books is a joint imprint of Little, Brown and Company and Warner Juvenile Books. This title is published in arrangement with Cloverdale Press Inc.

10 9 8 7 6 5 4 3 2 1

BP

For further information regarding this title, write to Little, Brown and Company, 34 Beacon Street, Boston, MA 02108

Published simultaneously in Canada by Little, Brown & Company (Canada) Limited

Printed in the United States of America

Interior design by Aisia De'Anthony
Interior illustrations by Diana Magnuson

ATTENTION!

All reader-players must read this page before the start of today's big game!

How many times have you watched a baseball game and thought, "What a dumb decision that manager made! What he *should* have done was . . . " Well, that's what this *interactive* book is all about.

There is an important ongoing baseball game taking place in this book, and as the manager of the home team, *you* must look at all the choices you have as the game goes on, make your own decisions and see what happens as a result. In this way, you don't read straight through as you would do with a regular story. Instead, each of your decisions will lead you to a new situation and eventually affect the outcome of the game. There are two voices in this book: yours (the manager's) and the announcer's. The manager sections will be in darker, bolder type.

Should you send the runner with the pitch? Should you play your infield in? Do you stay with your starting pitcher or bring in a relief pitcher? It's all up to you.

Follow the directions at the bottom of the page to guide you to the choice you want. At the end of the game, you can go back to the beginning of the book and try some different options. It will be a whole new ball game, because there are 26 different endings to the game! In some you win, in some you lose. How the game turns out is entirely up to you. So, play ball! Put on the old baseball thinking cap and get ready to guide the home team to victory!

OFFICIAL ROSTER

Your Opponents: The Springfield Hurricanes
Your Team: The Columbus Comets
Manager: _Justin Holland_

(Fill in your name or the name of your favorite manager)

Your Key Players:

Starting Lineup		Position	AVG	HR
1	Aaron "Flash" Parker	LF	.280	12
2	"Smilin' Lee" Balzano	2B	.270	8
3	Ken Cunningham "Sky King"	1B	.305	25
4	Graham Hatcher "Shakespeare"	SS	.315	28
5	Jim "Spark" McGreevey	C	.260	9
6	Bo "The Bopper" Brooks	CF	.271	23
7	Pete "Mac" MacKenzie	3B	.260	11
8	Web Lawrence "Spiderman"	RF	.260	18
9	Benny Barry "Wildcat"	P	.140	2
	OR			
9	T.B. Williams "Lefty"	P	.125	0

Pitchers	W-L	ERA	IP
Benny Barry/Righty "Wildcat"	19-7	2.67	230
T.B. Williams/Lefty	16-3	3.15	205
Nicholas Stanley/Lefty Reliever	7-2	1.95	77
Marty Braxton/Righty Reliever	8-3	2.15	65

The Announcer: <u>Jack Fartalot</u>

(Pick the name of your favorite announcer—from TV, radio or even your own neighborhood. Whenever you read the announcer's words in Play Book! Baseball 2, *imagine the announcer you picked as saying them.)*

RBI	SB	NOTES
40	31	Rookie; great base stealer
53	15	Good glove; good contact hitter
97	7	Hot bat; league leader in RBIs
89	12	Rookie phenom; he can do it all
57	9	Team captain; solid veteran
75	3	Power hitter
39	3	Popular veteran; having an off year
56	6	Big hitter; has been in a slump
5	0	Makes occasional contact
3	0	Shaky bat

SO	BB	NOTES
185	96	Rookie of the Year contender; fancy stuff; knuckler, good curve; moves the ball around a lot
176	51	Blazing fastball; sometimes takes a few innings to find his groove
65	29	Power pitcher; throws mainly strikes; 19 saves
41	36	Finesse pitcher; runs up a lot of full counts; 13 saves

Pinch hitters:		AVG	HR
Stan Olson/Lefty		.285	9
Ted Murphy/Switch-Hitter		.307	15
Ned Cypher/Righty		.286	13

Pinch Runner:			
Josh Franklin		.240	3

Starting Lineup for the Springfield Hurricanes	Position	AVG	HR
1 Chris Wilson	LF	.280	7
2 Steve Horka "Hollywood"	SS	.310	28
3 Ted Hartman	1B	.315	24
4 José Pina	2B	.250	25
5 Eubie Greene "Tater"	RF	.300	18
6 Mark Gearhardt "Sarge"	CF	.275	11
7 Carlos Rivera	3B	.265	6
8 Danny McCormick "Shotgun"	C	.240	1
9 Davey Michaels OR	P	.150	0
9 Mark Freeman	P	.180	2

Pitchers	W-L	ERA	IP
Davey Michaels/Lefty	16-6	2.69	219
Mark Freeman/Righty	23-8	2.90	240
Lefty Merryman/Lefty Reliever	5-3	2.25	90
Dave Cochran/Righty Reliever	9-4	2.15	110

RBI	SB	NOTES
49	9	Recent acquisition; good contact hitter
31	0	Power-hitter
59	5	Lots of pop in his bat, if not much spring in his step
7	18	Speedy; takes chances

RBI	SB	NOTES
38	23	Gets on base a lot
85	14	Great all-around player; hot bat
76	18	Having his best year ever at the plate
64	19	Great glove; struggling with the bat recently
53	4	Power hitter; always a threat
41	13	Fiery leader; plays aggressive ball
36	4	Good arm; so-so with the bat
6	0	Just up from the minors; big things are expected of him; fantastic arm
0	2	Strikes out a lot
4	0	Has occasional power

SO	BB	NOTES
110	65	Sidarm pitcher; great sinker and slider
151	50	Powerful fastball; good change-up
71	35	Throws his curveball when he's behind in the count; 21 saves
60	40	Fork ball makes him tough; 17 saves

*G*ood afternoon and welcome to Waverly Memorial Stadium, home of your very own *Columbus Comets!* This is your announcer, and I'm here to bring you all the play-by-play for the big one. That's right, it's the last game of the season and the amazing Comets are up against the powerful Springfield Hurricanes. It's hard to believe that the whole season has come down to this one game. But it has, and the winner of today's game moves on to the playoffs!

What a wild season the Comets have had this year. The club got off to one of the worst starts in its history, dropping the first 11 games in a row. Everybody thought the Comets were out of the running, but the team's owner decided to gamble and brought in a new manager. What an amazing job that young man has done! People have started calling him Mr. Wizard because his impact on this team has been nothing short of magical. The Comets broke out of their slump and romped over opposing teams for the rest of the season. Everything clicked.

And when the Comets started swinging their bats well, everything KABOOMED! Graham Hatcher, the Comets rookie shortstop, hit 28 home runs and drove in 89 runs. Those of us who appreciate the poetry of his glovework call Hatcher "Shakespeare." Like Shakespeare, Hatcher never makes a bad play. If everything goes as expected, we'll also be calling him the Rookie of the Year! Hatcher is a leading contender for that honor. Right behind Hatcher in the batting department is Kenny "Sky King" Cunningham, the Comets switch-hitting first baseman who knocked in 97 runs while pounding out 25 home runs. Seeing these two powerful bats back-to-back has struck fear in many opposing pitchers.

The Comets manager also got excellent work from some of the team's veterans. Longtime Comets, Jim "Spark" McGreevey and Bo Brooks combined for 32 home runs and 132 runs batted in. McGreevey had one of his best years as a catcher, nailing more than 40% of the runners who tried to steal second while he was behind the plate. Third baseman Pete MacKenzie has suffered some back problems but has still played most of the season. I expect you'll see Mac in there today: The Comets backup third baseman was just placed on the disabled list, leaving a hole in the roster.

But let's not pretend that these Springfield Hurricanes are going to roll over and die. The Hurricanes had a great year, jumping off to an early season lead and never letting go of it. Most of the team's success came behind the bats of first baseman Ted Hartman and Steve "Hollywood" Horka, the Hurricanes ever-dependable shortstop.

Looking out at the Columbus bullpen I see that the Comets manager has his two starting aces up and throwing. He hasn't yet announced which pitcher will start today's game; it's going to be a tough call. Mighty T.B. Williams, the Comets lefthander, would make sense. The Hurricanes have a lot of lefthanded hitters in their lineup and Williams has pitched well against them this year. But T.B. pitched a long game on the West Coast just two days ago and his arm is probably still tender after hurling fireballs all afternoon.

The other option, Wildcat Barry, the Comets rookie righthander, has had a little trouble with his control in his last few outings. When Wildcat is in a

2

groove, he can move the ball up and down, inside and outside, putting it anywhere he wants. When he has good control, he's nearly impossible to hit. If he were to have his best stuff today against the Hurricanes, I don't know about you, but *I* would be getting in line to buy my playoff tickets!

Well, would you look at this: Back at the start of the season, I was managing in the minor leagues. We traveled by bus; we stayed in lousy motels; we had nobody to clean our uniforms. . . . Now look at me. If I can get my team to win this one, we're in the playoffs. Wouldn't *that* be something! But if that's going to happen, I'm going to need my pitcher to be in control of this thing right from the start.

My best shot against this lineup would be Lefty Williams, but he's still a little sore. I could go with him and pull him at the first sign of trouble. But then there's Wildcat, who has had plenty of rest, although he might be wearing down a little this late in the season.

Well, the newspapers call me Mr. Wizard when it comes to making these kinds of decisions. Abracadabra . . .

▲ *To start Wildcat Barry, the rightbander, turn to page 4.*

▲ *To start T.B. Williams, the lefty, turn to page 46.*

3

The Comets manager is probably asking himself whether or not it was such a good move starting the righthanded pitcher Wildcat Barry against the Hurricanes lineup, which is mostly lefthanded. The Hurricanes hitters jumped on Barry for a single and a home run in the top of the first inning. Wildcat seemed to be trying to put too much on the ball—trying to throw it right past the batters. But the Hurricanes offense had no trouble with Barry, and we go to the bottom of the first inning with the hometown Comets trailing, 2–0.

Let's see what the Comets can put together against Hurricanes hurler Davey Michaels. Flash Parker leads off and draws a base on balls. Parker has hot feet, folks. He has already stolen 31 bases this year. I wouldn't be surprised to see the speedy leftfielder try to steal second base.

Lee Balzano is the next batter up for the Comets. Lee is a good contact hitter, but Michaels shows him a pair of blazing fastballs and a good-looking slider, and Lee goes down swinging.

That brings up the big bat of Kenny "Sky King" Cunningham. Cunningham brings a .305 average into today's game. He can hit it into the clouds if he gets his pitch. Out there on first, Parker is dancing off the bag. He is definitely ready to fly. Michaels goes into his stretch. Here's the pitch . . . . Sky King hits a towering ball out toward the leftfield wall! Parker got a great jump on the pitch and he is racing to second. The leftfielder, Wilson, goes back against the wall, looks up . . . . He's got it! Wilson fires the ball back

4

into the infield, trying to double up Parker, who is scrambling back to first. The relay throw is on its way to Hartman, the first baseman. Parker dives and slides into the bag head first . . . . He's safe by an inch!

Now there are two outs and one man aboard. Shakespeare Hatcher steps up to the plate. Parker is taking a long lead off first again. Michaels tosses the ball to Hartman to try to keep Parker close, but Flash is dancing off the bag. He'd love to steal second but he seems to be waiting for the green light from the bench.

Hatcher takes the count to three balls and a strike. A walk would put two men on base, but another out would end the inning. Maybe Parker should cool his jets out there at first for one pitch.

I'm two runs down already. I've seen how these Hurricanes operate. They get an early lead like this and they run away with the game. If only Sky King's blast had cleared the fence. Well, it didn't, and here we are.

The kid out there on first is fast. It's not an accident he's known as "Flash." Maybe I should give him the steal sign. But Shakespeare might walk and then I'd have Parker at second base anyway. What to do . . . ?

▲ *To have Flash try to steal, turn to page 6.*

▲ *To have Flash stay at first, turn to page 10.*

5

Hurricanes pitcher Michaels sets, checks Parker at first, and delivers. Flash Parker is gone!

Hatcher swings and misses. Danny McCormick, the Hurricanes catcher, fires the ball to second base. The throw is low and Pina, covering from second, takes it on the hop. That's all Flash needs. He slides under Pina's glove—safe! Stolen base number 32 for the speedy rookie. Hatcher lines the next pitch into right center for a base hit. Flash races from second and rounds third, his throttle open, and scores standing up. Parker set up that run with his steal of second base.

The next batter, Spark McGreevey, grounds a little roller out to the mound. Not much spark there, I'm afraid. It's an easy play for Michaels. The Hurricanes starter tosses the ball to first. Out number three. The inning is over, but the Comets did come up with a run. They now trail the Hurricanes, 2–1.

Both teams go scoreless in the second, but the Hurricanes add one run in the top of the third. Chris Wilson taps Wildcat Barry for a solo home run, making the score, 3–1. It seems Wildcat just hasn't found his groove yet. The Comets fail to respond in their half of the third, and soon they're in trouble again.

In the top of the fourth, José Pina leads off with a single for the Hurricanes, then advances to second on a sacrifice bunt. The Hurricanes have Sarge Gearhardt up now, and the veteran centerfielder has proven power. He fouls off the first three pitches from Barry, then watches two high ones go by for balls. That brings the count to 2-and-2.

Pina is taking a big lead out there off second. I wonder if the Comets are keeping an eye on him. Pina can really fly. It looks as if the Comets manager wants to have a word with Barry. The manager calls time and trots out to the mound. McGreevey, the catcher, joins the pair on the hill.

*L*ook, we can't let these guys open the game up on us. Can't we pick Pina off second base? He's taking a pretty big lead. I think he's ready to steal. Your pickoff move has gotten pretty good, hasn't it, Wildcat? But your move to second isn't as good as your move to first.

Hmm. McGreevey here thinks we should call a pitchout and just throw the ball out of the strike zone so he can fire the ball to third. If Pina tries to steal third, we should get him easily. If Pina doesn't run, McGreevey can still try to pick him off second. But maybe we should just ignore him. . . .

▲ *To throw a pitchout, turn to page 8.*

▲ *To pitch to the batter and hope for the best, turn to page 20.*

7

The Comets manager returns to the dugout. McGreevey, the catcher, goes back behind the plate. Pitcher Wildcat Barry looks in for the sign, goes into his stretch and delivers . . . . It's a pitchout! But Pina isn't running. McGreevey fires the ball down to Balzano at second. Pina dives back to the bag and just makes it. McGreevey almost picked Pina off and now the Hurricanes second baseman is taking a much smaller lead. Barry's next pitch is high for ball four.

That puts men on first and second with third baseman Carlos Rivera stepping up to the plate. Rivera is hitting .265 for the Hurricanes. Barry knows he has to pitch this guy carefully. He comes in with two twisting screwballs and Rivera flails at both for strikes. Barry misses the outside corner of the plate with his next two pitches, running the count to 2-and-2.

Barry checks the runners, then sets for the next pitch. He fires and Rivera swings. He hits a grounder down the third base line. Pete MacKenzie at third gobbles the ball up, touches the base ahead of the sliding Pina, and fires to second. Balzano, the second baseman, takes the throw . . . . Double play! The gamble paid off. Keeping Pina close to second base helps pull the Comets out of a jam.

We're in the bottom of the sixth inning now, and the Comets are still trailing, 3–1. Wildcat Barry seems to have found his groove. He has settled down the last several innings, holding the Hurricanes scoreless since the third and striking out four in the process.

Bo Brooks, the Bopper, steps into the batter's box

and then laces one into rightfield for a single. Hey, maybe this is the inning the Comets can get something going. Pete MacKenzie steps in. It was good to see Mac turn that double play back in the fourth. This hasn't been Mac's year; there has even been talk around the clubhouse of a possible trade during the off-season. It would be a shame to see this popular veteran leave the Comets. A timely hit here would certainly help his cause, not to mention the team's.

Traditional baseball wisdom says that MacKenzie will be up here looking to lay down a sacrifice bunt and move Bo Brooks over to second. But a look at the statistics shows us that over his career Mac has pounded Davey Michaels pretty well. Call me sentimental, but if I were running this club, I'd tell Mac to hit away.

If Mac was really hitting well, there would be no question about letting him swing away. This would be a great spot for a double—and old Mac used to really swat 'em.

But now, I don't know. That back problem really hurts his swing. If we're going to move Brooks over, I'll need a sacrifice bunt. Mac's a team player: He'd understand if I asked him to put it down.

▲ *To ask your ailing veteran for a sacrifice bunt, turn to page 19.*

▲ *To ask your hometown favorite to swing away, turn to 28.*

D avey Michaels, the Hurricanes pitcher, fires the ball over to first, but Flash Parker is just standing on the bag. It looks like the Hurricanes are going to try to keep him close. Michaels looks back to the plate. Shakespeare Hatcher, the batter, digs in. Michaels checks the runner again at first—Flash hasn't budged—then sets and fires.

Hatcher swings and chops the ball to the right of Horka at short. Horka makes a diving stab and comes up with the ball. His only play is at second base. Horka flips the ball to Pina, who beats Parker to the bag. It's too bad Parker wasn't running on the play. He probably would have reached second. So, credit Shakespeare with a fielder's choice.

In the third, the Hurricanes pick up two more runs, bringing the score to 4–0. It's been a rocky start here for Barry, the rookie who is definitely a Cy Young Award candidate. Only 21, Barry may be suffering a case of bad nerves in this life-or-death season finale. Or he may be just plumb tuckered out.

Of course, he could also use some support. The Comets go down without a fuss again in the bottom of the third.

We come to the top of the fourth inning with the hometown favorites still looking at a 4–0 score from the bottom. The Hurricanes are sending the top of the order to the plate. Coming into today, Chris Wilson, the Hurricanes leftfielder, was hitting .280 with seven home runs. Wilson is a good contact hitter with a high on-base percentage. Wildcat Barry leans in for the sign. He sets and throws . . . . Wilson swings and connects, sending a bounding ball back to the mound. The ball bounces off Barry's glove and rolls to the edge of the grass. Shortstop Hatcher scoops it up and fires off-balance to first. But the throw is wide and it pulls Cunningham off the bag at first. Wilson is aboard with an infield single.

This Wilson character on first sure can fly. He leads Springfield with 23 stolen bases. The next batter up, the lefthanded-hitting Horka, likes to pull the ball to rightfield. The Hurricanes third base coach looks like he's got fleas over there, he's flashing so many signals to Wilson across the way. I wonder if the Hurricanes are going to set Wilson loose.

The Comets manager is wondering, too. He's trying to signal his catcher.

Wilson likes to run, and that third base coach is giving more signals than a traffic light. If I have Spark call for a pitchout, maybe we'll nail Wilson trying to steal. Of course, if he's not running or if we don't throw him out, then I've put Wildcat behind in the count against one of the league's best hitters. Spark is looking over, I better give him a signal.

▲ *To throw a pitchout, turn to page 12.*

▲ *To skip the pitchout, turn to page 16.*

11

McGreevey wiggles his fingers, giving the sign to Barry. Barry sets and delivers. He throws a pitchout to the waiting McGreevey, who cocks his arm and . . . holds onto the ball. Wilson is hugging first base. Barry misses with a slider and falls behind, 2-and-0. Horka will now sit back and wait for his pitch.

Barry wheels and delivers. The lefthanded-hitting Horka sees a fastball he likes and slaps it into rightfield.

Web Lawrence comes in and scoops up the ball . . . . But look! Chris Wilson is trying for third. Who wound this guy up? Lawrence fires the ball into the infield. It's going to be close. MacKenzie's going to have to take it on the hop. Wilson slides . . . . He's safe!

Hartman, the next batter, lofts a long fly to center-field. Brooks makes the catch, but Wilson tags up and scores easily. Barry gets Pina and Greene on ground-outs to retire the side. But the Hurricanes have racked up another run and go ahead, 5–0.

In the bottom of the fifth, Spark McGreevey leads off with his 15th double of the year. Right behind him, Big Bo Brooks says, "Hey, me too!" and hits a double into the leftfield corner that scores McGreevey. Pete MacKenzie adds to the attack, lining a shot down the rightfield line that scores Brooks from second. That's all for Michaels, the Hurricanes starter. Righthander Davey Cochran comes in and gets the 'Canes out of the inning without further damage.

In the bottom of the sixth, the Comets look like they're going to rally again. Lee Balzano gets a base on balls and then moves to second on a wild pitch. Cochran gets Cunningham to pop out to Pina at second. Up comes Shakespeare Hatcher. Shakespeare fights off a few pitches and then lines one into left center for a double. Balzano streaks around third, into home, and right into the dugout. It's a good thing there isn't a backdoor to that dugout, or Balzano would have gone all the way out to the parking lot!

So that closes the gap a bit, making the score 5–3. Hatcher, like Balzano before him, stands at second, waiting for someone to bring him around. McGreevey steps up. Don't let that .260 average fool you. This is the guy who got the rally started in the last inning. He's always been good in the clutch. A hit to almost any field would have a chance to score Hatcher. Here's the pitch. . . . McGreevey loops a fly ball into shallow rightfield. Hatcher holds at second in case it's caught.

No! The ball drops in front of the rightfielder, Greene. Hatcher takes off! Greene bobbles the ball for a second. Hatcher is charging for third. The Comets manager is out of the dugout. I can't believe it! Are they going to wave him on?

C ome on, Shakespeare! *Hustle!*

OK, he's going to make it to third. Should I tell him to keep running or hold him up?

▲ *To wave the runner around third, turn to page 14.*

▲ *To hold the runner up at third, turn to page 15.*

13

They're waving Hatcher around third! Greene finally finds the handle on the ball and fires it toward the plate. McCormick, the Hurricanes catcher, is out in front of the plate, blocking it. Hatcher comes in like a bull . . . and BAM! The two go down. Dirt flies everywhere. I see Hatcher's hand on the plate . . . and the ball on the ground! Hatcher knocked it out of McCormick's glove. Hatcher scores, cutting the Springfield lead to 5–4.

In the meantime, McGreevey went to second and is standing there with his helmet off, enjoying the lovely view. But not for long. Brooks drives McGreevey in on the next pitch, tying the score, 5–5.

The Comets add a go-ahead run in the eighth inning. In the ninth, the Hurricanes go down one, two, three. The crowd is going mad as Barry blows a fastball by the final batter for strike three. The Comets win! They move on to the playoffs!

Didn't I tell you this was going to be a perfect afternoon for baseball?

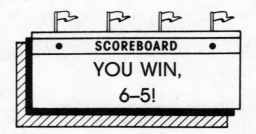

SCOREBOARD

YOU WIN,
6–5!

Hatcher steams into third. He makes the turn at third, but at the last second the third base coach *and* the manager put up the stop sign. Hatcher skids on the dirt and hurries back to the bag. But McGreevey has been fooled. He figured the play would be at the plate and now he's hung up between first and second base. The second baseman chases McGreevey back toward first, pumps twice, then tosses the ball to Ted Hartman, the first baseman. McGreevey squirms to avoid the tag, but he doesn't have a chance. He's out!

Hatcher has broken for the plate! Hartman fires the ball to the catcher, McCormick. The throw beats the runner by a good four steps. Hatcher slides, but he too is an easy out. The double play kills the rally, and at the end of six, it's 5–3, 'Canes.

In the seventh, the Hurricanes chase Barry to the showers with another run. It's the final run. The Hurricanes come out on top, 6–3. The only way the Comets will get to the playoffs this year is to buy a ticket. Tough luck, guys. See you next year.

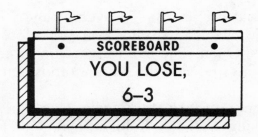

SCOREBOARD

YOU LOSE,
6–3

McGreevey turns his gaze from the dugout to the mound. Barry looks in for the sign. He sets, then throws to the plate. Horka chases a sinker in the dirt. McGreevey blocks the pitch with his chest. It would have been a great pitch for the fleetfooted Wilson to be running on, but he's sitting tight at first. Wilson may have figured that the Comets would try a pitchout early in the count.

The catcher, McGreevey, returns the ball to Barry. Barry checks Wilson at first, turns back to the plate and fires. Horka swings and bounces a chopper into the gap between first and second. Cunningham's there. He gobbles it up, turns to his right and throws to Balzano at second for one. Balzano fires it to Barry, who is covering at first. Wildcat takes the toss and touches the bag . . . in time! Double play!

Hartman then flies out to centerfield to end the inning. Balzano hits a solo home run in the fifth inning to give the Comets their first run. Barry puts the Hurricanes down in order in the fifth and sixth innings. In the bottom of the sixth, we're still looking at a 4–1 game. The Comets are hoping this will be their big inning.

Bo Brooks brings his .271 average and 75 RBIs to the plate. Michaels' first pitch comes in close . . . and hits Brooks. Ouch! The ball caught him on the shoulder. Bo seems fine, and the umpire sends him down to first base.

That brings up Pete MacKenzie. Mac lashes the first pitch for a single. Brooks holds up at second. Suddenly

16

there are two runners on and nobody out. The crowd jumps to life! Can you hear them? Now *this* is what they came for!

Web Lawrence steps in and goes down swinging. He can't seem to find his timing, and it just got kind of quiet around here.

Wildcat Barry is the batter due up. The last time I saw Wildcat hit the ball was about two months ago when he was ducking out of the way of a pitch. The Comets manager has plenty of good hitters sitting on the bench . . . . Maybe it's time to use one.

It would be a shame to see a second out now. If I let Wildcat bat, I can pretty much chalk up a "K" on my scorecard. I mean, my mother can hit better than this guy. Hey, but can my mother throw a sinker, slider, fastball? Hmm, I don't know. I haven't asked her lately. But in the meantime . . .

▲ *To let the pitcher bat, turn to page 22.*

▲ *To put a pinch hitter in for the pitcher, turn to page 18.*

It looks like the Comets manager has decided to go for the big inning. He has called Wildcat Barry back to the dugout and he's sending up a pinch hitter. It's Ted Murphy, the switch-hitter. Murphy is batting .307 this year, with 15 homers and 31 RBIs. He'll be batting righthanded against lefty Davey Michaels.

The outfielders shift toward left for the big slugger and they stay deep. Here comes the pitch. Murphy pulls one down the leftfield line. It's fair! The ball rolls into the corner. Leftfielder Chris Wilson runs over to dig it out. Brooks scores from second. MacKenzie scores right behind him. Wilson is still having trouble digging the ball out of the corner. Murphy is trying for three! Wilson's throw from the corner is . . . late! Murphy slides into third with his fifth triple of the season. The Comets are behind by one run, at 4–3! A great pinch-hitting effort by the veteran Ted Murphy.

Unfortunately for the home club, the score remains the same for the rest of the game. The Comets bring on a new pitcher, Nick Stanley, their lefthanded stopper. Stanley doesn't let a runner aboard, but even that doesn't help. The Comets fail to bring in any more runs and lose the game, 4–3.

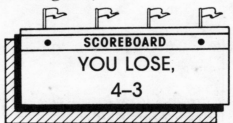

SCOREBOARD

YOU LOSE,
4–3

*P*ete MacKenzie approaches the plate. The first pitch is a ball. Here comes the second pitch . . . . MacKenzie lays one down! It's a gem. McCormick fields the ball and has no choice but to throw to first. Big Bad Bo Brooks cruises into second on the sacrifice, giving the Comets a runner in scoring position. The crowd gives Mac a nice hand as he heads back to the dugout. Sure, a double would have been nice, but the veteran MacKenzie knows there's more than one way to be a hero.

MacKenzie's sacrifice, however, doesn't lead to a run. Bo Brooks grows old out there on second as his teammates fail to knock him in. The Comets come up empty-handed in the sixth.

The Hurricanes add an insurance run in the top of the seventh, making the score, 4–1, and sending Wildcat Barry to the showers. The Comets bring Nicholas Stanley, their leading reliever, in from the bullpen to see if he can put a lid on the Hurricanes attack.

Stanley turns in a couple of fine innings in relief. But to win the game, you've got to score runs, and the Comet bats were as quiet as a library today. The Comets lose the season finale and come up just one game short of making the playoffs.

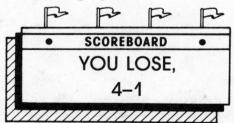

SCOREBOARD

YOU LOSE,
4–1

The Comets manager returns to the dugout after his conference. The pitcher, Barry, looks in to his catcher for the sign. Barry sets and fires . . . . The runner on second, Pina, takes off! Gearhardt swings and slaps the ball down the first base line. The first baseman, Ken Cunningham, dives for the ball and keeps it from going through, but Gearhardt beats him to the bag. Pina holds up at third.

That brings up the Hurricanes third baseman, Carlos Rivera. Barry will want to pitch him carefully. The last thing they want is . . .

It's a hit! Rivera lines one into shallow center. Bo Brooks, the centerfielder, dives for it and misses. Pina will score from third. Flash Parker races over from leftfield and fields the ball. Gearhardt is trying for third! Parker hurls the ball to MacKenzie at third . . . . Not in time! Gearhardt is safe. Rivera is trying for second on the throw. Mac throws to Balzano, who makes the tag. Rivera is out, but the Hurricanes have scored another run. The Comets now trail, 4–1.

Barry walks McCormick and Michaels to load the bases. The Comets manager is on the dugout steps watching his pitcher carefully. Relief pitchers Stanley and Braxton are up in the bullpen. But Barry works his way out of the inning, striking out the leftfielder Wilson to end the inning.

The next few half-innings pass uneventfully. In the bottom of the sixth, Spark McGreevey leads off with a walk. That brings up Bo Brooks who has been hitting the ball well lately. He would love to move

McGreevey over. He takes a cut at an outside pitch and loops it into shallow right for a base hit. That moves McGreevey to second.

MacKenzie goes down swinging, then throws his bat down in disgust. Up next is Web Lawrence, who has gone hitless in his last 14 at bats. Lawrence hits a chopper right back to the mound. Michaels takes the ball and throws over to third to force McGreevey.

The next batter up is the pitcher, Wildcat Barry. He has bounced back from a shaky fourth inning with two hitless innings, but I'm not sure if Barry is worth keeping in the game at this point. This is about the closest thing to a rally the Comets have had since the first inning.

I *have* to get some runs out of this thing. I know that Wildcat would like to stay in and pitch. He's young. It would be a real boost to his confidence if he hung in there and we were able to get out of this game alive. On the other hand, I'd hate to strand my two runners. . . .

▲ *To put a pinch hitter in for the pitcher, turn to page 18.*

▲ *To keep the pitcher in and let him hit, turn to page 26.*

21

Apparently, Barry is going to stay in and take his swats. He stands in, knocks the dirt off his cleats, then digs in to face Michaels. Michaels throws—and Barry bunts. He taps a gem down the third base line! Rivera charges in from third and bare-hands the ball. No one is covering third. Brooks will make it safely to the bag. The only play is at first. Rivera throws off balance . . . and he throws wide! The ball bounces into foul territory!

Andy Kelley, the third base coach, waves Brooks home. There is no play at the plate. Brooks scores. MacKenzie is hustling for third and Barry scoots into second. I don't think Barry has ever even *seen* second base!

Take a moment to catch your breath, folks. Just who invented this crazy game, anyway! The Comets have closed the gap to 4–2. Out on the mound, Davey Michaels doesn't like this turn of events one bit. There is steam rising off his forehead. Next up is Flash Parker. Michaels rears back and fires . . . . The ball hits the plate and bounces over McCormick. Wild pitch! Parker is waving MacKenzie in from third. He scores standing up. The Comets have cut the Springfield lead to one run.

The Hurricanes manager trudges out to the mound. He's making a pitching change, bringing in righthander Dave Cochran.

Cochran can't stem the flood. The hometown boys score two more runs. The Comets go into the seventh inning leading, 5–4.

Steve "Hollywood" Horka leads off the Hurricanes half of the seventh. Hollywood has been held hitless so far today. The Comets infield is playing Horka straight away. He steps in and jumps on the first pitch. A line shot over second base. Balzano leaps to his right . . . and stabs it! It's an amazing leaping catch that robs Horka of a hit. I'm telling you, with Smilin' Lee out there, you might as well hang up a sign that reads: "Don't Bother Trying."

The next batter, Ted Hartman, squeezes a walk out of Barry. That brings up José Pina. Pina is only a .250 hitter, but is an excellent bunter. And Hartman on first has wheels, too. He has 19 stolen bases this year.

Here comes the Comets manager to the mound. Spark McGreevey joins him there.

O K now, we've got to play this right. The best thing would be to double this Pina guy up. But if we play him at double-play depth and he ends up laying down a bunt, Hartman over there will be standing on second. And I don't want that. What do you think, Spark? Do you think we should play him at double-play depth and try to get him to hit one on the ground, or do you think we ought to move in and guard against the bunt?

▲ *To play the batter at double-play depth, turn to 24.*

▲ *To play the batter to bunt, turn to page 40.*

23

The Comets infield settles in at double-play depth. The pitcher, Wildcat Barry, fires one toward the plate. Pina raps the ball directly at Hatcher at short. Hatcher flips the ball to Balzano covering at second. Balzano jumps over the sliding Hartman and gets his throw off to first . . . in time! Double play! The inning is over.

The eighth inning is uneventful. Barry retires the first two 'Canes in the ninth. Another out and he'll take home his 20th victory of the season—and send his team to the playoffs!

Steve Horka steps up to the plate. Horka can hurt you, and nobody knows that better than Wildcat Barry. Horka has tagged Barry for three home runs already this season. Barry sure doesn't want to make it four right now.

Barry looks in for the sign. He winds and fires toward the plate. Horka swings and sends a towering shot to deep leftfield. Uh oh, this could be trouble. Parker goes back . . . back . . . he's on the warning track . . . . He's got it. Out number three. The Comets win! Players on the field and then from the dugout mob Wildcat Barry. Now they have their manager up on their shoulders. What a game!

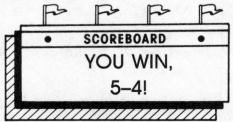

SCOREBOARD

YOU WIN,
5–4!

25

It looks like Wildcat Barry is going to bat after all. Barry, hitting a lean .140, takes a few lame practice swings. The runners take their leads. Here comes the pitch . . . . Both runners go. Barry swings and misses. McCormick fires the ball down to third. The throw is high and Brooks slides in safely. A double steal! That didn't just catch the Hurricanes off guard, it caught everyone in the stadium off guard!

Now the Comets have a potential run just 60 feet away. The pitch comes in to Barry. He turns to bunt it down the first base line, but he hits it instead on one bounce back to Michaels, who throws over to first to retire the side. So the Comets strand two and head to the seventh trailing, 4–1.

The Hurricanes start off where the Comets left off, sending their pitcher up to the plate. Michaels isn't a bad-hitting pitcher. He steps in against his counterpart and laces a hit just over the grasp of MacKenzie at third. Michaels takes first and Barry shakes his head in frustration. He must be wishing *he* had delivered a single his last time at bat.

Next up is Chris Wilson, the Hurricanes leftfielder. Wilson is a hot hitter with men on base. Chris looks at a pair of strikes and then hits a slider to the hole at second. Balzano jumps on it, but he has no play at second. He throws to first base to get Wilson.

This brings up Hollywood Horka, the Hurricanes powerful shortstop. Horka is hitting .310, with 85 RBIs and a league-leading 38 doubles. With the wind gusting as it is, Horka is very dangerous. The Comets trail, 4–1, in the seventh. The Comets manager must be wondering whether his club should pitch to Horka or issue him a pass to the vacancy at first by walking him. This could be a great game for second-guessers, who are already having a field day with the manager's decision to let Barry bat for himself in the sixth.

I can't believe I let Barry bat last inning. That might have been my best chance to get some runs. And now look. His arm is tiring anyway. I should have pulled him.

Well, I didn't, and here we are. I don't even have a pitcher warmed up in the bullpen, so I'll have to let Barry pitch to Horka. But maybe we ought to just play it safe and walk him. Who do they have up next? Hartman. He's hitting .315. Can't a guy get a break? These Hurricanes keep bringing it at you.

Well, I've got to do something. . . .

▲ *To walk the batter intentionally, turn to page 35.*

▲ *To pitch to the batter, turn to page 36.*

*B*rooks takes a short lead off first. There's not much of a chance he'll try to steal. He has only stolen second three times all season. The Springfield pitcher, Michaels, takes a look at Brooks, then brings the smoke to the plate. Mac swings. He strokes a line drive over the head of the leaping shortstop. Base hit! Brooks got a good jump from first and he's rounding second, digging for third. Mark Gearhardt in center charges the ball. He throws and . . . Brooks slides . . . . Safe! Gearhardt's throw was high and Bo slid under the tag. Mac started to head for second on the throw but had to hold up and retreat to first. That hit had to feel good for the old vet.

That puts men at the corners, with Web Lawrence coming to the plate . . . . No. It looks like the Comets manager is going to make a change here. Yes, he is sending Ted Murphy up to the plate. The switch-hitting Murphy will also take Lawrence's spot in right-field. The Comets manager must figure that Murphy, who is batting .342 as a righthander, has a better chance against the southpaw Michaels than the left-handed Lawrence had. Murphy looks at two called strikes, then sends a booming shot into the leftfield seats. A home run! Murphy turns the game upside down with his 16th home run of the year. The Comets now lead, 4–3.

In the top of the seventh inning, the Comets cling to a 4–3 lead. The Hurricanes manager sends up a pinch hitter to lead off the inning. Barry works care-fully—perhaps too carefully—as the batter draws a walk. Barry did not want to walk the leadoff hitter, particularly when he's trying to protect a one-run lead.

Next up is Carlos Rivera, the Hurricanes third baseman. Carlos loops the first pitch into shallow left-field. Parker races in and fields it on the bounce. The runners hold at first and second. And suddenly, the Comets are in a hole. The Comets manager has Nick Stanley, his lefty reliever, warming in the pen. It's possible that Wildcat is starting to tire. He has already thrown nearly 90 pitches.

I t might be time to change pitchers. Ninety pitches, a leadoff walk and Rivera's Texas Leaguer to left. Wildcat may be running out of gas. I've got Stanley warmed up and ready to come in if I need him. But this is Wildcat's game. He's trying to win his 20th. Maybe I should let him try to get out of this hole on his own. On the other hand, we have a playoff spot at stake. . . .

▲ *To bring in the reliever, turn to page 30.*

▲ *To keep your pitcher in, turn to page 32.*

*S*o, that's it for Wildcat Barry today. But Barry will still get the win if Nick Stanley can close the gate on the Hurricanes right now.

Stanley halts the Springfield threat in the seventh and puts the Hurricanes down in order in the eighth. In the top of the ninth, still protecting a 4–3 lead, Stanley gets the first two batters to fly out to center-field. Stanley walks two straight batters, but he falls behind on the next hitter, three balls and a strike.

Stanley asks the umpire for a new ball. The left-hander rubs the ball down a bit, then looks in for the sign. He shakes off three times, then steps off the rubber and picks up the rosin bag. He looks up into the stands, pounds his cleats against the rubber, tugs on his cap, squares his shoulders and leans forward. He comes to the stretch . . . and the pitch. . . . It's swung on and hit high in the air to the gap between leftfield and center! Parker and Brooks are racing over for it! Oh, no! I don't think they see each other. They collide in the gap. Both men are down.

But Parker has the ball! He held onto it! The game is over! Columbus has gone from last place to first place, and the Comets are in the playoffs!

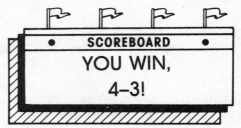

SCOREBOARD

YOU WIN,

4–3!

The Comets manager has had a talk with his pitcher and it looks like he has decided to keep Barry in. This is going to be Barry's game to win or lose.

Next up is the Hurricanes catcher, Dan "Shotgun" McCormick. This young player is just up from the minors. The Comets haven't seen him enough to really know how to pitch him. He is only hitting .240, but the Hurricanes manager has chosen to go with McCormick in the most important game of the season. That's some vote of confidence. If Barry can get past McCormick, he'll probably face a pinch hitter for Michaels, the Hurricanes pitcher.

Barry throws a slider, a sinker and a change-up, and the rookie fans on three pitches. Beautiful pitching! Barry must have told the skipper that his arm was still feeling *very* good.

And as suspected, the Hurricanes are sending up their pinch-hitting slugger Ned Cypher to bat for the pitcher, Michaels. Barry isn't out of this yet. He jams Cypher on the inside and gets him to chop the ball to the shortstop, Hatcher, who scoops the ball up and throws to MacKenzie at third for the force. Two down.

The Hurricanes still have men on first and second and Wilson, the next batter up, takes Barry deep, sending a home run into the Comets bullpen. Wilson's blast puts the Hurricanes ahead, 6–4. Barry gets Horka to fly out to rightfield to end the inning.

We're in the bottom of the eighth. The Hurricanes still lead, 6–4. Parker leads off and draws a walk. He tries to steal and McCormick guns him down at second.

Well, now we know about the arm on the Hurricanes catcher. McCormick has a bazooka. No, correct that. It's a shotgun!

Next up is Smilin' Lee Balzano. Lee has a great eye. He rarely strikes out. The feisty second baseman fights off a couple of pitches until he finds the one he wants, then he smacks the ball right by Hartman at first for a single.

That's going to bring up Kenny "Sky King" Cunningham, the league leader in RBIs. The Hurricanes obviously respect Cunningham's power. The outfield has moved back about 10 feet and the infielders are playing just off the outfield grass. I guess they expect Cunningham to clobber the ball.

It's late in the game and they're up by two. After seeing Parker get cut down trying to steal, I'd better not try the same thing with Balzano. I guess the best thing is to let Kenny swing away and hope for the best. Hey, wait a minute. Look how far back they're playing him. It's crazy, but I wonder if I should tell my slugger to lay down a bunt. That would fool a few people, wouldn't it? Of course, if it didn't work, I'd be hearing about it all winter long.

▲ *To have Cunningham swing away, turn to page 34.*

▲ *To have Cunningham bunt, turn to page 42.*

33

Here's the pitch. Cunningham drives a fly ball deep into the corner. Rightfielder Eubie Greene is racing over, but he's not going to get to the ball in time. It drops for a hit! Balzano races around second and is headed for third. Greene is having some trouble digging the ball out of the corner. Cunningham is legging for second. Balzano rounds third. There's going to be a play at the plate! Greene hits Hartman, who spins and fires to McCormick. Balzano goes in headfirst and knocks McCormick over just as the ball gets to the plate. Balzano is safe, and Columbus cuts the lead to 6–5!

Cunningham and Hatcher also score before the inning ends, giving the Comets a 7–6 lead. They hold onto their one-run edge in the ninth and head for the playoffs!

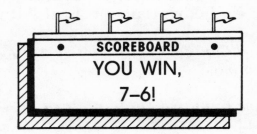

SCOREBOARD

YOU WIN,
7–6!

Wildcat Barry, the Comets pitcher, throws four balls, giving Horka a pass to first. That brings up Ted Hartman. Barry takes a long look at Horka over at first, then comes to the belt and fires the ball to the plate. Hartman swings and connects. The ball is hit into shallow center. The centerfielder, Brooks, is coming on hard. . . . The ball is dropping. . . . Brooks dives . . . . He doesn't get it! Base hit! Michaels and Horka held until they were sure Hartman's liner would fall. They move to third and second, respectively, and the bases are loaded, with the 'Canes second baseman, José Pina, coming to bat. The Comets still aren't warming anybody up in the bullpen. It looks like they plan to stick with Barry. Wildcat looks in for the sign and pitches . . . Good night, grandma! It's out of here! Pina sent that pitch screaming over the leftfield fence. A grand slam, the first of the season for the Hurricanes cleanup hitter. The 'Canes take an 8–1 lead.

Flash Parker and Ken Cunningham hit back-to-back doubles in the bottom of the ninth to start a last-gasp rally. But it's not enough. The next three hitters pop out and that's the end of the game. Hey, let's call it like it is. That's the end of the *season!* Better luck next year!

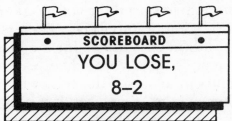

SCOREBOARD

YOU LOSE,
8–2

*C*atcher Spark McGreevey gets a signal from the bench, calls time and goes out to the mound to confer with his pitcher, Wildcat Barry. They must be deciding on how they're going to pitch to Horka. Or *if* they're going to pitch to him.

McGreevey goes back behind the plate and gives Barry the target. Barry paints the inside corner of the plate for a called strike. Barry's next pitch is in the same spot, but it sinks just as Horka takes a cut at it. Strike two.

Horka steps out of the box. He is talking to himself. Barry has thrown him two great pitches. Folks, you're looking at the reason this rookie pitcher has won 19 games. Horka steps back in. Barry throws a change-up, which Horka pops up to the third base side. Horka throws his bat to the ground as MacKenzie settles under the ball. Mac hauls it in and suddenly there are two outs. Personally, I thought they should have intentionally walked a big slugger like Hollywood Horka. And personally . . . I was wrong.

Barry gets Hartman to ground out to second to end the inning.

In the bottom of the seventh, the Comets still trail, 4–1. Parker steps in to start things off. Parker, a rookie, was hitting .280 coming into today. The first-year outfielder has a youthful enthusiasm for the game. Parker is one of the team's most vocal cheerleaders.

Parker stands in against Michaels, who winds and delivers. Parker swings . . . and sends it back, way back . . . . Tell it good-bye. Home run number 13 for

Parker. It's a lucky 13 for the Comets, who cut the lead to 4–2. Parker is not in the dugout to lead cheers, but his teammates are yelling just the same.

Next up is Balzano. Smilin' Lee doesn't have much to smile about this turn at bat as he strikes out swinging. One away.

Here comes Cunningham. Ken has hit Michaels well in the past. He swings at the first pitch and hits a line shot to Rivera at third. Rivera can't find the handle. He drops the ball, picks it up and then throws wide to first, pulling Hartman off the bag. Cunningham reaches base on the error.

Hey, this game isn't over yet!

All right! We're still in this! Who would have figured a homer from the leadoff hitter? I'll have to buy the kid a pizza after the game. That ought to make him happy.

Now what should I do about Sky? It's late in the game, there's one out and we still trail. Kenny has such a sure glove at first base that I would hate to pull him out now for a pinch runner. I might need his glove in the eighth and ninth.

But I still need a few runs. And Sky isn't exactly the fastest man on my team.

▲ *To keep Cunningham in, turn to page 38.*

▲ *To put in a pinch runner, turn to page 39.*

Apparently the Comets manager is going to keep Kenny Cunningham in the game. I guess he figures he might need his defense—and his bat—later on. Up next is Graham Hatcher, currently hitting .315.

Here comes the pitch . . . . Hatcher lays a bunt down the first base line. Hartman, anticipating the bunt, charges from first. He grabs the ball but collides with the pitcher, Michaels, who also went for the ball. Hartman spins, tags Hatcher and then turns and throws to Horka at second . . . in time to double up the slow-footed Cunningham. It's tough-going for the Comets, who trail, 4–2, at the end of seven.

The Hurricanes pick up another run on a single and a double in the top of the ninth inning. The Comets send three men up in their half of the ninth and the Hurricanes, just as quickly, set them down. Let me tell you folks, it is a quiet crowd at the old ballpark today. The Comets finish a great season, but come up a game short when it really matters.

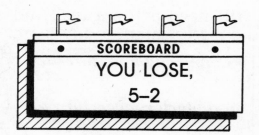

SCOREBOARD
YOU LOSE,
5–2

Josh Franklin goes in to run for Cunningham. Franklin's a speedy youngster. He has stolen 18 bases on 22 tries. Shortstop Graham Hatcher is up. Here comes the pitch . . . . Hatcher taps a beauty of a bunt toward third. Catcher Danny McCormick bare-hands the ball and throws it to second. The speedy Franklin beats the throw. Pina whips the ball down to Hartman at first but Hatcher crosses the bag just ahead of the throw. Both runners are safe! Good thing they put the speedy Franklin in—Ken Cunningham would have been cut down on that play for sure.

That brings up Jim McGreevey. The count goes to 2-and-1 and then McGreevey hits a shot over the bag at second and into centerfield. Franklin is rounding third. He'll score! Hatcher digs for third. He slides in safely. McGreevey holds up at first.

Brooks steps into the batter's box with runners on the corners. He looks at a pair of strikes, then lifts the next pitch high into the air out toward left. Kiss that one good-bye! That's home run number 24 for "The Bopper." The Comets take the lead, 6–4.

Brooks's home run puts the Comets ahead to stay. They win, 6–4, and advance to the playoffs.

SCOREBOARD

YOU WIN,
6–4!

Pina steps in and takes a couple of vicious cuts. He doesn't look like he's thinking "bunt." The Comets infield is on the edge of the grass, guarding against a possible bunt. With the infield in, Pina will find it easier to hit one through the defense, if he swings away. The Comets are up by one here in the seventh, but Springfield is looking to piece something together.

The pitcher, Barry, takes a look at the runner at first, then delivers the pitch. Pina squares to bunt. He taps a roller down the third base line. MacKenzie races in, fields the ball and goes for the lead runner at second. But his throw bounces in front of Balzano and gets by him. Hartman hustles to third.

The Comets had the defense set perfectly for the play but MacKenzie's throw was two feet short. The next batter up, Greene, lofts a long, high fly ball to deep rightfield. Lawrence nestles under it for the second out. Hartman tags up and scores easily. The Hurricanes tie the game, 5–5. Barry gets Gearhardt to ground out to first to end the inning.

The Hurricanes pick up another run in the bottom of the eighth on a solo home run by Carlos Rivera. The Comets go quietly in their half of the eighth. Barry retires the side in order in the top of the ninth. So the Comets are down to their last three outs and still trail by one.

Balzano leads off and hits the ball sharply to the second baseman, who fumbles with it just long enough for Balzano to beat the throw to first. It's an error on the second baseman, Pina. Balzano advances to second on a sacrifice bunt from Ken Cunningham. I'm surprised the Comets manager took the bat out of his slugger's hands. The Comets are truly playing for the one run. Graham Hatcher steps up. Cochran intentionally walks Hatcher to set up a possible double play.

So now we take a look at McGreevey.

He steps in with two on base. It's suddenly very quiet here in the stadium. For McGreevey, it's now-or-never time.

Here comes the pitch . . . . It's outside, but McGreevey lunges for it and pokes a single over the head of the first baseman. Balzano was running with the pitch. He'll score easily, and that ties the game. Greene throws to third base, where Hatcher slides in safely. McGreevey takes second on the throw. The crowd is on its feet!

Bo Brooks is up next. Bo hangs his bat out over the plate and takes a few powerful swings. Cochran, the Hurricanes stopper, has been in this type of situation all year. Bo waits for the pitch. It comes in letter high and he strokes the ball cleanly into leftfield, scoring Cunningham from third! The game is over! The Comets win the division with a stunning comeback victory.

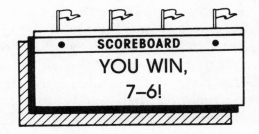

SCOREBOARD

YOU WIN,
7–6!

*C*unningham turns as if to bunt on Cochran's first pitch, then pulls back and takes a called strike. You've got to wonder. The Columbus slugger bunts once in a blue moon. Was he just trying to draw the infield in to give him more room to poke the ball through? Could be. If Cunningham really is up there to bunt, that would be one of the season's bigger surprises. Cunningham slides the bat into bunting position again on the next pitch. Cochran's fastball is high and Cunningham backs off. McCormick whips the ball down to Hartman, but Balzano is back to the bag safely.

Cochran delivers again . . . and Cunningham is actually bunting. He lays the pitch down the first base line. Cochran, McCormick and Hartman all rush to the ball and then wait for it to roll foul. But the ball swerves away from the foul line, back toward the field. Cunningham is on with a bunt single.

Hatcher steps in to face Cochran. Shakespeare sends Cochran's first pitch into the rightfield corner. Balzano scores easily. Kelley, the third base coach, waves Cunningham around third. Greene's throw to the infield is wild. Cunningham scores, and the game is tied, 6–6.

The Comets score one more run in the eighth and carry their one-run lead into the top of the ninth. The Hurricanes get a man on second, with only one out. Tater Greene is up to bat. Barry throws three straight balls to Greene. Barry isn't even near the strike zone. Wildcat has become just that—wild. He has put in an awfully long afternoon. This will be all for the rookie righthander. The Comets manager takes the ball from Barry and the crowd gives Barry a well-earned hand.

The Comets manager has a lefthander, Nick Stanley, and a righthander, Marty Braxton, warmed up in the bullpen. The Columbus skipper is talking now with his catcher, Spark McGreevey. They're probably sizing up the next couple of Hurricane hitters.

OK, we've got both Stanley and Braxton warmed up. Do you think we ought to go with the southpaw or bring in the righthander? No, Spark, I don't want you to decide. That's what they pay me for. It's time to start earning my keep.

▲ *To bring in the righthander, turn to page 44.*

▲ *To bring in the lefthander, turn to page 53.*

The Comets manager signals for the righthander. That means we'll take a look at Marty Braxton. Braxton is a finesse pitcher who uses an assortment of pitches and all of the strike zone.

Braxton works the count full—three balls and two strikes—gets Tater Greene to ground out to the shortstop, Hatcher, who looks Hartman back to second base before throwing the ball to Cunningham. This brings Sarge Gearhardt to the plate. Braxton's first pitch is outside for a ball. Braxton shakes off a couple of signs from McGreevey, then gets set to throw. Ball two. He goes into the stretch again and delivers. He just misses the inside corner. Ball three. It's nail-biting time.

Braxton is searching for the strike zone, but he hasn't found it yet. Here is the 3-and-0 offering . . . . Gearhardt, with the green light, swings and sends a high pop-up into foul territory. The ball looks like it's going to land in the first few rows of seats. The catcher, McGreevey, races to the railing. McGreevey knows the ball tends to come back toward the field. McGreevey lunges for the ball and goes right into the seats! The umpire runs to the rail. McGreevey jumps up and holds his mitt up with the ball in it.

But the umpire is not going to allow the catch. Apparently, he thinks one of the spectators helped McGreevey snag that pop-up. Here comes the Comets manager. He is furious!

What do you mean, "foul"? My man caught the ball. Nobody touched it! Do you need new glasses! The batter should be out! *I* say so, that's who. What do you mean, one more word and I'll be out of the game?

The Comets manager is furious, but he backs down before getting thrown out of the game.

Gearhardt steps back into the batter's box. The count is three balls and one strike. Braxton throws him a slider. Gearhardt swings and misses. I can see the big grin on the Comets manager's face from up here. Gearhardt now has a full count, three balls, two strikes, two outs. Gearhardt likes the next pitch and swings. He sends it into deep rightfield. Rightfielder Lawrence goes back. He looks over his shoulder for the ball and leaps . . . . He's got it! He robs Gearhardt of a home run! Lawrence's amazing catch ends the game, saves the win and sends the Comets on to the playoffs!

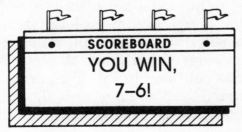

SCOREBOARD
YOU WIN,
7–6!

1 t looks like the lefthander, T.B. Williams, is getting the nod. Williams has an ERA of 3.15. He has 16 wins this season and, remarkably, only three losses. He has struck out 176 and walked only 51. His success is due largely to his great fastball. It's a heater that has hitters all over the league talking to themselves.

Earlier the Hurricanes manager was saying that if the Comets decided to start Williams today, the Hurricanes would come out swinging. They know that T.B. is almost always around the plate. The Hurricanes will try to counter Williams's aggressive pitching with some aggressive batting.

Let's see what they can do. The Hurricanes send Chris Wilson, their leftfielder, to the plate to lead off. A .280 hitter, Wilson swings at the first pitch of the game and lines the ball into shallow center for a single. Now, that's not a bad way to get things going . . . unless, of course, you're a Comets fan.

Next up is Steve "Hollywood" Horka, the Hurricanes hard-hitting shortstop. Hollywood is batting .310 with 28 home runs and 85 RBIs. Williams throws a fastball down the middle for a strike . . . and Chris Wilson steals second! The Comets catcher, Spark McGreevey, didn't even get off a throw. Yes, sir, it looks like the Hurricanes mean business today.

Williams sets for his next pitch. Here it comes . . . . Horka swings and hits the ball down the leftfield line. It's a fair ball! It rolls into the corner. Wilson is steaming around third. He'll score without a play! Hollywood holds up at second base with a double and an

RBI. The Hurricanes waste no time, grabbing a quick 1–0 lead.

And that brings Ted Hartman up to the plate. Hartman, who plays first base for the Hurricanes, is enjoying one of his best years ever. Ted comes into the game today hitting .315. He has hit a career-high 24 home runs and knocked in 76 runs. He is certainly capable of inflicting more damage here—and that's just what Williams has to avoid. The Comets need to get out of this hole before it gets any deeper.

Not good, not good. These Hurricanes can tear you up if they get a decent lead on you. They're playing aggressively, that's for sure. They're swinging at the first pitch, stealing bases. . . . Now what should I do about Hartman? This guy has one of the liveliest bats in the league these days. Maybe I ought to give him an intentional walk and give us a chance for a double play. After all, first base is empty. But then again, this is the first inning. Maybe a free pass would look like they've got us running scared already. . . .

▲ *To give Hartman an intentional walk, turn to page 48.*

▲ *To pitch to Hartman, turn to page 54.*

The Comets give Hartman a free ticket to first base. That puts two men on with no outs and one run already in.

Next up for the Hurricanes is their second baseman, José Pina. Williams looks in for the sign, kicks and fires. He throws a fastball down the middle. Pina gets a piece of it and punches the ball over Cunningham's head at first. Horka charges around third base and is going to try for home. The Comets rightfielder, Web Lawrence, charges the ball and fields it with his bare hand. He throws a rocket to the plate. McGreevey steps in front of the plate . . . . Here comes Hollywood . . . . Here comes the ball . . . . He's out! McGreevey makes the tag. What a great play!

The heads-up Ted Hartman moves over to third on the play. Pina motors to second. The next batter up is Eubie "Tater" Greene. Greene hits a sacrifice fly to deep center. Hartman tags up and scores. Williams settles down and gets the third out. But the Hurricanes, who came out swinging, lead after just half an inning, 2–0.

The score remains unchanged through the second inning. The Hurricanes pitcher, Mark Freeman, has a little trouble in the third inning. The Comets pick up a run with some alert base running by Lee Balzano who singles, steals second base and then takes third on Freeman's wild pitch. Graham Hatcher drives Balzano home with a single, then is thrown out trying to stretch his hit into a double.

In the bottom of the fourth, the Comets still trail by

one. The leadoff batter, Spark McGreevey, legs out an infield hit. That brings up Bo Brooks, the man with a tree in his hand. Bo is batting .271 and has 23 homers and 75 RBIs. So what in the world is he doing on the first pitch? He squares to *bunt* and takes a called strike one. What is *that* all about?

A ha! That surprised them, didn't it? No one expected my power-hitter to be thinking bunt. But we need to move McGreevey over to second somehow. I really ought to let Bo swing away. That would be the normal thing. But now I'm not sure . . . . I kind of like keeping these Hurricanes off balance when I can.

▲ *To have your power-hitter bunt, turn to page 50.*

▲ *To let your batter swing away, turn to page 60.*

49

*B*rooks takes a few strokes, then settles back into the box. The Hurricanes infield is playing him straight away. They're betting that the Comets centerfielder is going to swing away. In my book, that's a good bet.

So much for my book! Brooks lays a perfect bunt down the third base line. Freeman charges off the mound and fields the ball. But he is off balance and he hurries his throw to first. The throw sails over the first baseman! Brooks chugs into second. McGreevey cruises into third. Everyone is safe! Having Brooks bunt certainly defied every normal baseball convention, but it also caught the Hurricanes leaning back on their heels.

Pete MacKenzie comes up to the plate next. He raps a single into leftfield and drives in McGreevey. Listen to that crowd now! Freeman is unraveling a bit. The Comets have tied the score and are looking to go ahead. Web Lawrence grounds back to the mound. Freeman freezes Brooks on third before throwing Lawrence out at first. MacKenzie moves to second base. Freeman then fans Williams and gets Parker to pop out to Pina at second to end the inning.

But the Comets have battled back. It's all tied up!

It's the sixth inning now, with the score still tied, two apiece. With one out, the Hurricanes send their rookie catcher, Danny McCormick, to the plate. Williams struck McCormick out his first two times up. Lefty winds and throws. The pitch is high and tight. It hits McCormick on the shoulder. McCormick appears to be all right as he jogs down to first, glaring at Williams the whole way. Hey, he got put on base. Maybe McCormick should thank the guy!

Or maybe I should clam up.

OK now, the Comets have a decision to make. The next batter is the Hurricanes pitcher, Mark Freeman. So if you ask me, we're looking at a bunt, all the way. After all, Freeman is hitting .180. Think about it. Would *you* tell him to aim for the fences?

The Comets infield is playing up on the grass. McCormick has pretty good wheels for a catcher. He stole 18 bases earlier this year while still down in Triple A. With the Hurricanes playing for the bunt, McCormick is taking a good-size lead. You have to wonder if the Comets are keeping enough of an eye on him.

I f Freeman bunts, the easy out is at first. But that puts their catcher on second, and with his speed he can score on almost any ball to the outfield. We really ought to try to go for the lead runner on the bunt. But if we don't get him, then there will be two on and just one away. I don't like that scenario one bit. Let's see, what's the best way to play this one. . . ?

▲ *To go for the lead runner on the bunt, turn to page 52.*

▲ *To go to first on the bunt, turn to page 66.*

51

Mark Freeman squares to bunt. He taps a beauty down the first base line. The Comets catcher, Jim McGreevey, pounces on it. He fields the ball and fires a rocket down to the shortstop Hatcher, covering second. Hatcher takes the throw and floats across the top of the bag for out number two. It was a heads-up play by McGreevey. Wilson singles to leftfield, but Parker nails Freeman trying to go first-to-third, and the top half of the sixth is over.

In the eighth inning, it seems someone has lit a *fire* under the Comets offense. Aaron Parker, the left-fielder, plugs a two-run homer, which is followed with a solo blast by Kenny "Sky King" Cunningham that sends Freeman to the showers.

But the relief pitcher, Lefty Merryman, isn't much relief either. The Comets rock him with back-to-back doubles by McGreevey and Brooks, and a broken-bat single by Pete MacKenzie, the Comets veteran third baseman.

When the dust clears, the Comets have scored five runs in the eighth. Their 7–2 win, my friends, sent your very own Columbus Comets on their way to the playoffs!

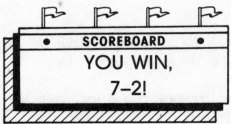

SCOREBOARD

YOU WIN,
7–2!

After talking it over with his catcher, the Comets manager has given the nod to his lefthanded relief ace, Nick Stanley. Stanley has an ERA of 1.95. He has won seven, lost two, and comes into the game with 19 saves.

Stanley inherits Barry's count on Greene, three balls and no strikes. There is one out and Hartman, the Hurricane runner on second, is in scoring position.

Stanley throws. The ball threads the middle for a called strike. Stanley gets the ball back from McGreevey and immediately goes to work again. Greene fouls the next pitch back into the seats. Have a souvenir, folks. The count is full, three balls and two strikes. Stanley rears back and fires. Greene swings and misses, strike three. The Comets are one out from victory.

It all comes down to Sarge Gearhardt, the Hurricanes centerfielder. But Stanley is untouchable. He blows three sizzlers by Gearhardt, who strikes out to end the game.

That's it! The Comets hold on to win it by a score of 7–6. Nick Stanley gets the save, and Wildcat Barry picks up his 20th win of the season. We'll see you at the playoffs!

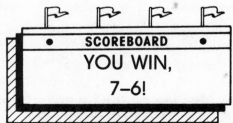

SCOREBOARD
YOU WIN,
7–6!

*C*omets pitcher T.B. Williams looks in for the sign. He throws a fastball right down the middle. Hartman jumps on it and slaps a chopping grounder past the third baseman for a single. Leftfielder Parker charges the ball and keeps Horka from coming around to score. Williams then walks Pina and loads the bases.

Up next is Eubie "Tater" Greene. Greene, a .300 hitter, is a lefthander who can really pull the ball. Williams pitches. Greene hits a ball just out of the reach of the diving Cunningham. Horka will score . . . Hartman will score. The Hurricanes take a 3–0 lead.

In the bottom of the fourth, the Comets still trail, 3–0, and they really need to get something going. Williams leads off and pops one up to the catcher, McCormick, back by the seats. One away.

That brings up the top of the Comets batting order, Aaron Parker, the Flash. And as his nickname tells you, he is *fast.*

Parker hits a high chopper out toward short. Horka lets the ball play him and has to back up and take it on the hop. He hauls it in and throws to first—but Parker has already crossed the bag! There aren't many people who can get down the line as fast as Parker.

Lee Balzano, the Comets second baseman, is up next. They call him Smilin' Lee because the one thing he *doesn't* do during the game is crack a smile. Balzano is 100% concentration, 100% business. He fights off a couple of inside pitches, then sends a boomer out to centerfield. But Mark Gearhardt has played him perfectly and is right there to make the catch. Balzano certainly isn't smiling as he hustles back to the dugout.

Two outs now and Kenny "Sky King" Cunningham is coming to the plate. Parker is taking a pretty good lead off first. Trailing by three and with the league's best RBI man up, I doubt the Comets manager wants to cut him loose. Then again, with an inoffensive attack so far, the manager may be looking to stir something up. . . .

W e're down by three. My fastest man is on first and my best hitter is at the plate. Hey, things could be worse.

But I'm not sure I should let Parker try to steal second. Why chance it, with a bat like Cunningham's ready to let loose? If they cut Flash down stealing, we're out of the inning.

▲ *To let the runner try to steal, turn to page 56.*

▲ *To hold the runner on first, turn to page 64.*

Hurricanes pitcher Mark Freeman throws over to first, trying to keep Parker close. But the moment the ball is back to the mound, Parker dances off the bag again. Hartman can't worry just about Parker, he has to be concerned about a ball hit in the gap between first and second.

Freeman goes into his stretch and makes his pitch . . . . Parker is going. The Hurricanes have a pitchout! McCormick comes up firing, shooting the ball down to Pina at second. Parker dives and slides headfirst into the bag . . . . Safe! What amazing speed!

Cunningham comes through, too, rapping the next pitch into leftfield for a single. Parker was running on the pitch, and he makes it home easily. The Comets are finally on the board. They now trail, 3–1.

The Comets add a run before they're finished in the fourth and then two more in the fifth. We've come to the top of the sixth with the score, Comets four, Hurricanes three. The Hurricanes lead off with a pair of singles and the Comets manager replaces pitcher T.B. Williams with another lefthander, Nick Stanley. The hard-throwing Stanley has a terrific fastball and an effective sinker. Stanley's ERA is an impressive 1.95 and this season alone he has racked up 19 saves.

The first batter Stanley will face is Eubie "Tater" Greene. Tater has knocked in two of the Hurricanes three runs today. He has the hot bat. The Comets will have to play heads-up ball to keep their lead. . . .

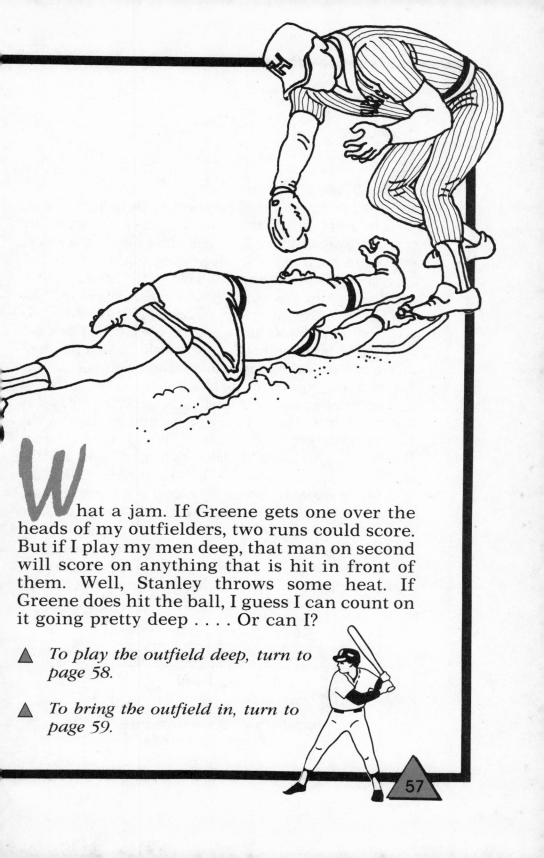

What a jam. If Greene gets one over the heads of my outfielders, two runs could score. But if I play my men deep, that man on second will score on anything that is hit in front of them. Well, Stanley throws some heat. If Greene does hit the ball, I guess I can count on it going pretty deep . . . . Or can I?

▲ *To play the outfield deep, turn to page 58.*

▲ *To bring the outfield in, turn to page 59.*

Stanley has finished his warm-up tosses and Eubie Greene steps in to bat. It looks like the Comets are protecting against the long ball. The Comets manager is playing his outfield straight away and deep.

Stanley comes in with his hard stuff. Strike one! He checks the runners and delivers the next pitch . . . . Strike two! Greene took a home-run cut and corkscrewed himself into the ground. We clocked that last pitch at 94 miles an hour. With a ball thrown that fast, and Greene's sweeping swing, if he makes contact the ball is going to go into orbit.

Here comes the next pitch . . . . Greene swings. He hits a towering fly ball into deep centerfield. But the Comets manager has his outfield positioned perfectly. Brooks is right there. He takes two steps back onto the warning track and hauls it in. The runner on second tags up and takes third as Brooks throws into second. Stanley retires the next two Hurricanes batters and the Comets leave the inning with their lead intact.

Stanley is superb in relief. He stops the Hurricanes cold. Not a single Hurricanes player reaches base after Stanley comes in. Behind his pitching, the Comets come out victorious. They win the game, 4–3.

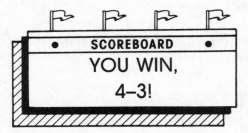

SCOREBOARD

YOU WIN,
4–3!

58

Stanley finishes his warm-up tosses and the catcher, Spark McGreevey, trots out to the mound for a conference. They want to be careful about how they pitch to big Tater Greene. McGreevey signals to the outfielders. He wants them to come in about 20 feet. McGreevey seems to think he and Stanley can get Greene to hit the ball where they want.

They're wrong. Greene lifts the first pitch into deep centerfield, over the head of Brooks. One run scores. Brooks races after the ball. He chases it down and fires it to the cut-off man, who spins and throws the ball to the plate. The throw is too late and another run scores.

Greene ends up on second base with a stand-up double. Tater has knocked in four of the Hurricanes five runs today. It looks like he'll be winning the Comets MDP award, Most *Difficult* Player!

The Comets get a single from pinch hitter Stan Olson in the ninth. But it's too little, too late. The Comets come up short. It's a lousy end to a great season.

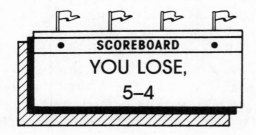

SCOREBOARD

YOU LOSE,
5–4

The Hurricanes infield isn't quite sure now how to play the mighty Mr. Brooks. They just can't believe he would really bunt. And he doesn't. He sends a sharp grounder into the gap between short and third! Horka makes a diving stab and comes up with the ball! He flings it to Pina at second, who scrapes the bag with his foot, then fires down to first . . . in time! Double play!

That will bring up third baseman Pete MacKenzie. Freeman challenges Mac with a pair of fastballs, then changes him up and gets a swinging third strike. The Hurricanes are out of the fourth holding onto their one-run lead.

That score holds for another inning. Then, in the top of the sixth, T.B. Williams, the Comets pitcher, finds himself struggling again. Centerfielder Mark Gearhardt leads off with a single. He is followed by Carlos Rivera, who slaps the ball into shallow center-field, where Bo Brooks fumbles the sinking liner. Rivera reaches first base on the error, and Gearhardt races to third.

That brings up Dan McCormick, the Hurricanes rookie catcher. Williams throws a pair of pitches out-side for balls. On Williams's third pitch, Rivera takes off for second. McGreevey fires down to second . . . and now Gearhardt takes off from third! A delayed double steal! Rivera slides hard into second, knocking Balzano off balance before he can throw the ball to the plate. Gearhardt scores! The Hurricanes take a 3–1 lead. One pitch later, McCormick gets a free pass to first base. That brings up the Hurricanes pitcher, Mark

Freeman. Williams throws him four straight balls to load the bases. You hate to walk the pitcher, particularly in this situation.

The Comets manager is heading out to the mound. It looks like he wants to have a talk with his big left-hander.

Williams, what in the world is the idea of walking their pitcher? That guy is hitting .180! Now level with me. Is your arm tired? We can't let these guys score any more runs. I've got Braxton ready in the bullpen. Do you think maybe you should just call it a day? I know, *I'm* the manager. . . .

▲ *To pull the pitcher out, turn to page 72.*

▲ *To keep the pitcher in, turn to page 62.*

*I*t looks like T.B. Williams is staying in. With nobody out and the bases loaded, Chris Wilson, the Hurricanes leadoff hitter, comes up. Williams sets and fires. He hits a sharp grounder through the legs of the first baseman. Rivera will score from third and McCormick is right behind him. Lawrence charges the ball in right-field. Wilson is trying for second. Here comes the throw from Lawrence . . . . Hatcher puts the tag on Wilson. He's out! Now here comes Freeman. Hatcher hurries a throw to the plate . . . but it's too late. Freeman is safe. The Hurricanes score three runs on one batted ball! Williams finally has empty bases again. He winds and throws a waist-high fastball to Steve Horka. Horka hits a towering home run to left center! Williams was left in the game not one but two batters too long, and now the Hurricanes lead, 7–1.

Things only get worse in the seventh, with the Hurricanes roughing up first reliever Marty Braxton then Nicky Stanley who surrenders two more runs. The Comets go down in order in the ninth and go off to a winter vacation that will be haunted by the nightmare that was lived out this afternoon.

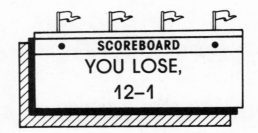

SCOREBOARD

YOU LOSE,

12–1

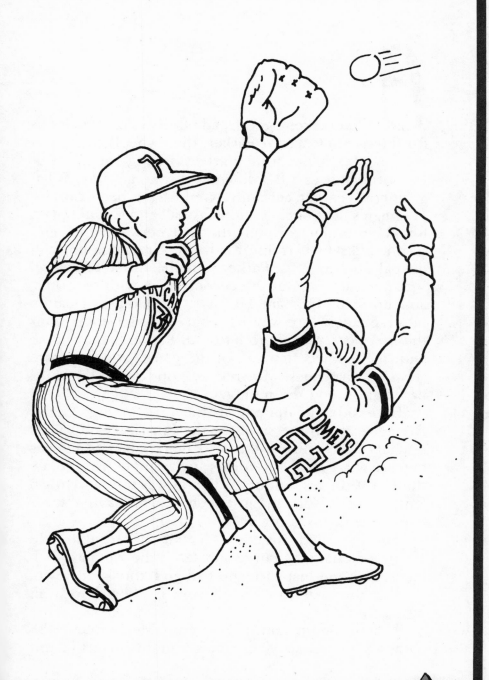

Flash Parker takes a good lead off first. Freeman looks for the sign, glances at Parker, then wheels and delivers . . . It's a pitchout. Parker is snug on first but McCormick fires a BB down to second anyway. What a cannon! Parker certainly would have been caught. Freeman's next pitch is a low fastball and Cunningham hits a grounder through the gap between first and second. Parker is trying for third. Greene is up with the ball and fires . . . . Parker slides headfirst. He's safe!

There are men at the corners now with two outs, and up steps Graham Hatcher, the Comets cleanup hitter. Shakespeare waves his bat in the air, then sends the first pitch sharply to leftfield. Parker scoots home with the Comets first run of the game, and the score is 3–1, Hurricanes. McGreevey pops out to the third baseman to end the inning.

Both sides go quietly in the fifth inning. Carlos Rivera leads off the sixth for the Hurricanes. Comets pitcher T.B. Williams throws Rivera a pair of pitches that are w-a-y inside. Rivera is angry and he yells something at Williams. I doubt Williams was trying to brush Rivera back. Williams just seems to be having some trouble with his control.

But the riled Rivera is having no trouble. He swings at a hanging curve and sends the ball past Williams. Balzano leaps for the ball and knocks it down, but his throw is too late. Rivera is aboard with an infield hit.

That brings up Danny "Shotgun" McCormick. Williams's first pitch to McCormick is in the dirt. Williams looks in for the sign. He shakes off a couple of pitches, then finds one he likes . . . and McCormick likes it, too! McCormick hits a chopper right over the head of the leaping Williams. Again, Balzano pounces on it. He shovels the ball to Hatcher who is covering second. But Hatcher juggles the ball long enough for Rivera to reach second safely. There is no throw to first. Hatcher has been given an error for bobbling the ball. There are two men on and nobody out.

T.B. Williams is really getting into a hole here. He looks in to see Mark Freeman stepping to the plate. Freeman is only batting .180. But Williams walks Freeman, sending him to first and bringing the Comets skipper jogging out of the dugout.

Has your arm turned to rubber? You can't go nibbling around the strike zone with these guys! You have to throw strikes! I don't know about you, but I'm not ready to start my winter vacation just yet.

I'm awfully glad to hear you're not either. So you just loaded the bases because you thought it might make things more fun? Maybe I should pull you out now and bring Stanley or Braxton in. What do *you* think?

▲ *To keep the pitcher in, turn to page 62.*

▲ *To pull the pitcher out, turn to page 74.*

The Comets infield creeps in toward the plate as Williams goes into his stretch. Here comes the pitch . . . . Freeman squares to bunt. He lays down a beauty along the first base line. Ted Hartman roars in and scoops it up. He fires the ball to Balzano, who moved over to cover first. They get Freeman at first. McCormick holds up at second. Nice play by Hartman.

Chris Wilson steps up to the plate and fights off the first two pitches, sending them foul. Shotgun McCormick is taking a pretty good lead off second. The Comets don't seem to be paying attention to him. Williams's next pitch is a change-up . . . and McCormick takes off! By the time the ball reaches the plate, McCormick is standing on third base, waving his helmet to the booing crowd. Wilson knocks Williams's next pitch into rightfield. McCormick jogs home with the go-ahead run.

Horka smashes a scorcher to the third base side. Mac handles it like a pro. Hey, he *is* a pro! MacKenzie throws the runner out at first. The inning is over but not before the Hurricanes take a 3–2 lead.

In the bottom of the seventh, it looks as if the Comets manager has decided to get aggressive. His pitcher, Williams, was due to lead off here in the seventh, but still trailing 3–2, the manager has decided to send in a pinch hitter. It's Stan Olson, a recent acquisition who hasn't seen much action for the Comets. Olson dusts off his bat and delivers a single to left. Just what the doctor ordered!

That brings up the top of the order, leftfielder

Aaron Parker. Parker brings *two* bats to the plate and steps in. The crowd loves his act! They're chanting "Two! Two! Two!" The umpire, however, doesn't love it. He tells Parker to lighten his load. With only one bat in tow, Parker returns and looks at a couple of outside pitches. Then he lines the next pitch to short. Horka lowers his glove, but the ball takes a bad hop and hits him in the face. Horka goes down! Olson sees this, and he rounds second, hops over the Hurricanes shortstop and races on to third.

Wait! The umpire at second base, Frank Guerra, is calling Olson out! He is signaling that Horka had the ball in his glove and that he tagged the runner on the foot. The Comets manager comes running out onto the field. He is yelling at his base runner to stay on third. He's charging over to Guerra. Boy, is he steamed!

You must be out of your mind! My man is safe! He cleared that guy by a mile! There's no *way* that guy tagged him out! You've been out here in the sun too long!

What do you mean if I keep this up, I'm not going to be out here in the sun *at all?* You will not throw me out of the game! Yeah, I say so. I'll say one more word if I please. . . .

▲ *To keep arguing with the umpire, turn to page 68.*

▲ *To give up the fight and go back to the dugout, turn to page 70.*

One more word and I'm out of this game? One more bad call like you just made and my *team* is out of this game!

That does it for the Comets skipper. Second base umpire Frank Guerra has just given him the heave-ho. He turns away from Guerra . . . and leaps over Steve Horka, who is still down on the ground.

Did he tag me? Am I out?

He's out all right. So now, let's see. Where were we? Oh, yes, a baseball game. OK, Olson is out, and Parker is safe on first. The Comets third base coach, Andy Kelley, will take over as acting manager. On the next pitch, Kelley gives Parker the green light to steal second. But McCormick guns Parker down with another impressive throw.

At the end of the game, it looks as if the Comets manager is going to spend his winter wishing he had held his tongue in the seventh. The Comets fell apart here in the last couple of innings. A pair of untimely Comets errors and a timely home run from Hurricanes José Pina brought the curtain down on the Comets season. Kelley, the acting manager, just couldn't seem to make any good decisions. This team really needed Mr. Wizard today. So the Comets finish the season on the short end of a 5–2 score.

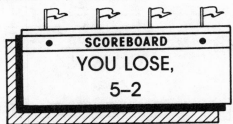

SCOREBOARD

YOU LOSE,
5–2

I don't know what Guerra, the second base umpire, just said, but the Comets skipper suddenly gave up his argument and is returning to the dugout. And he's taking Olson. That leaves Parker on first looking antsy and Balzano coming to bat. Hurricanes pitcher Mark Freeman looks to the batter. He rocks and fires . . . . Parker goes! Balzano sends the ball over the head of the leaping third baseman and into leftfield. Parker is around second and digging for third. Wilson has trouble coming up with the ball. The Comets manager is waving his arm from the dugout. He wants Parker to try for home. Here comes the throw. . . .

Safe! Parker hook-slides around McCormick's tag and across the plate. What a gutsy move! It's a good thing the Comets manager didn't get tossed from the game. Parker might have held at third if his boss hadn't been waving him on!

Freeman gets out of the inning without further damage, but the Comets have tied it up, 3–3.

The Comets pick up another run in the eighth to break the tie. They're off to the playoffs!

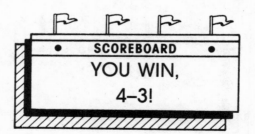

SCOREBOARD

YOU WIN,

4–3!

That's all for Williams. He gave up three runs in five-plus innings and is responsible for the three Hurricanes now filling the bases. The Comets new pitcher is Marty Braxton. Braxton has 13 saves this season as well as eight wins, three losses and a sparkling 2.15 ERA.

Don't look for Braxton to throw too many pitches down the middle. He's a finesse pitcher who likes to spot the ball. Chris Wilson steps into the box and Braxton greets him with a dancing screwball. Wilson swings at it but isn't even close. Braxton works again, throwing a slider that just nips the outside corner of the plate. Strike two. Wilson has been a productive hitter with men on base, so Braxton can't give him anything too good with the count 0-and-2. Braxton winds and delivers . . . a sinker that dips out of the strike zone. Wilson holds off and then chases it with a lunging swing. Strike three! Woe to the impatient hitter who faces Braxton.

Braxton works his magic on the next two batters. He strikes out three straight hitters with the bases loaded. Now *that's* relief! But the Comets need more than good pitching—they need runs. In the bottom of the sixth, they still trail, 3–1. Cunningham goes to the plate and grounds out to second. Hatcher follows with a pop-up to the third baseman. Two quick outs.

Spark McGreevey steps to the plate. A spark is exactly what the Comets need right about now. Bo Brooks is on deck, swinging three bats at once over his head. If McGreevey can get on, Brooks would represent the potential tying run.

The Comets catcher crowds the plate. He fouls off

the first four pitches Freeman throws. It looks like McGreevey is trying to wear down the Hurricanes pitcher. Here comes the next pitch . . . . McGreevey swings and connects, busting his bat into two pieces. The fat end hits Bo Brooks right in the head! He's down! The ball drops into shallow rightfield for a broken-bat single.

The Comets team doctor rushes onto the field to have a look at Brooks. The big centerfielder is up on one knee. He is shaking his head to see if anything is loose. That chunk of timber really nailed him. I'm not sure he'll be able to stay in the game.

Here comes the Comets manager now to take a look at his player.

Bo, are you OK? Where did it hit you? No, I know you were in the batter's box. I mean, where on your head did it hit you? Are you seeing double? How many fingers am I holding up? Can you tell if it's two or four? No? This is terrible. McGreevey's on first. We need your bat. I don't want to pull you out of the game.

No, I can't just aim you toward the plate— you're seeing double. I need you to hit a double, not see double.

▲ *To keep Brooks in, turn to page 77.*

▲ *To take Brooks out, turn to page 78.*

73

The Comets manager has sent Williams to the clubhouse and brought in Marty Braxton out of the bullpen. The righthanded reliever has 13 saves to his credit and an ERA of just 2.15. He'll be facing Chris Wilson, the Hurricanes leadoff man. Wilson's average coming into today was .280, but it is even higher with men on base. And, boy oh boy, are there men on base!

Braxton knows that with the bases filled he can't be too cute with Wilson. He has to throw strikes.

Wilson hits the first two pitches from Braxton back into the stands. The Columbus infield is in close for a possible play at the plate. The Comets need Wilson to hit the ball on the ground. Braxton delivers the pitch . . . . Wilson stings a sharp grounder to Hatcher at short. Hatcher scoops up the ball and fires to the plate for one. McGreevey wings the ball down to first . . . . Double play! Excellent work by the Comets defense.

The Hurricanes have men on second and third. Hollywood Horka steps to the plate. Horka, hitting .310 at the start of today, was once on the same team as Marty Braxton back in the minor leagues and supposedly they were real pals. Braxton sets and delivers . . . . His pitch is in the dirt at Horka's feet. It gets by McGreevey and McCormick dashes home to make the score 4-1.

Horka trips and falls on his way to first base. He was busy watching his former teammate and he didn't keep an eye on where he was going. Braxton grabs the ball and throws him out. This could be the end of a beautiful friendship.

In the bottom of the seventh, the Comets still trail, 4–1. Their manager needs to find a way to get his team back into this game. Hatcher leads off and flies out to rightfield on the first pitch. It isn't a promising start for the home club. That brings up catcher Jim McGreevey. McGreevey looks at two strikes, then raps a double to leftfield. *That* looks more promising.

Bo Brooks is up next. Brooks has been hitting Freeman well all season long. Freeman confers with McCormick. It looks like the Hurricanes are going to intentionally walk Brooks to set up a possible double play and to keep Brooks from knocking one out of here. Wait! The Comets manager comes out of the dugout and runs over to Brooks. He wants to have a few words with his slugger.

Maybe you should swing at the ball. I know they're throwing it out of the strike zone but this might be our only chance to get some runs. Just reach across the plate and swing at anything close. Perhaps you'll catch them on their heels.

The only problem is that a pitch that far out of the strike zone is going to be tough to get good wood on. Hmm, should you swing or not?

▲ *To have Brooks swing at anything, turn to page 80.*

▲ *To accept the walk, turn to page 76.*

The Comets manager finishes his conference with Brooks by shaking his head "no" and heading back to the dugout.

Freeman throws four balls well out of the strike zone and Brooks is given the intentional base on balls. That brings up Pete MacKenzie, with two on and one out. MacKenzie grounds a Freeman fastball down to Pina at second. Pina flips the ball to Horka, who fires to first . . . . Double play! The Comets rally fizzles and they end the seventh down, 4–1. Springfield clings to its lead and wins.

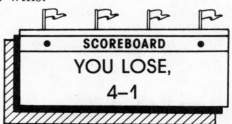

SCOREBOARD

YOU LOSE,
4–1

Brooks was hit pretty hard by the flying bat, but the Comets manager has decided to keep him in the game. The crowd cheers as Brooks steps up to the plate—facing the wrong direction! He's just kidding around, folks . . . I hope. Samuelson, the home plate umpire, laughs and turns Brooks around.

On the mound, Mark Freeman isn't laughing. He throws an off-speed pitch way outside, to see if Brooks might chase a bad one. And he does! Bo steps over the plate and smashes the ball over the 385-foot mark in rightfield. It's a home run! The crowd is on its feet! McGreevey comes in to score. Brooks trots around the bases, waving his helmet in the air. But crossing third he trips over the bag and goes down hard! He gets up and stumbles the rest of the way to home plate, but he's obviously hurt and his skipper is pulling him out of the game. It's all even at three apiece.

Pete Mackenzie follows Brooks to the plate. The veteran third baseman, bothered by back pain, has had an off-season. He lofts a Freeman fastball into the air. The wind is taking it back, back . . . . It's a home run! Back-to-back home runs! The Comets take the lead and hold on to win, 4–3!

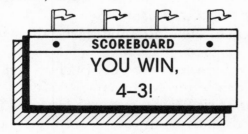

SCOREBOARD

YOU WIN,
4–3!

*B*rooks seems to want to stay in the game, but the Comets skipper has decided to take him out and put in lefthanded swinger Stan Olson, instead. Olson is batting .285 with 49 RBIs. McGreevey is standing on first base, yelling at Olson to hit him in.

Hurricanes pitcher Freeman checks the runner at first, then delivers a waist-high fastball to the plate . . . . Olson tags it! Horka dives for it at short, but the ball is by him and into leftfield! Leftfielder Wilson overruns the ball and has to backtrack to retrieve it. McGreevey is headed for third . . . and Andy Kelley, the third base coach, is waving him on.

Wilson gets to the ball and makes a hurried throw that goes wide of the plate. McCormick moves off the plate to catch it. McGreevey scores on a single by Olson and the error by Wilson. The injury to Brooks certainly hasn't been the undoing of the Comets.

Up next is Pete MacKenzie. Olson, who advanced on Wilson's throw, is at second. Mac's bat has been pretty quiet lately. He would sure love to make some noise with it right now. Freeman hangs a curve out over the plate and Mac rips into it. The ball screams into the gap in left center for a double. Olson scores from second to tie the game, 3–3.

It's the top of the ninth inning, and the game is still tied at three apiece.

Marty Braxton, the Comets pitcher, gets McCormick and pinch hitter Ned Cypher to fly to Parker in leftfield, but Chris Wilson tattoos a fastball for a single to right. Wilson is followed by Hollywood Horka, who also singles off Braxton, with Wilson holding at second base. Braxton throws a wild pitch and both runners move up a base. Braxton seems to be tiring. With first base now vacant, the Comets decide to walk Hartman, loading the bases.

It is as quiet as a library in this stadium right now. We're in the top of the ninth and the bases are loaded. There are two outs and the game is all tied up.

Hartman steps in. He shades his eyes and looks out at the men on the bases. He cocks his head, then raises his bat over his shoulder. Comets pitcher Marty Braxton delivers a strike to the inside corner. Hartman taps his bat on the plate and sets for the next pitch. It comes in at the knees for a called second strike. Braxton comes to the belt, then unloads the pitch . . . BOOM! Ted Hartman got all the wood on that one. Centerfielder Brooks is going back . . . . back . . . He is at the fence . . . . He leaps . . . . Home run! Ted Hartman clears the bases with his 25th home run of the season and probably the biggest home run of his career! Oh my goodness, what a difference a hit makes! The Hurricanes leap out in front, 7–3.

The Comets go down quietly in their half of the ninth. It is going to be a long winter for the home team.

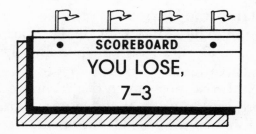

SCOREBOARD

YOU LOSE,
7–3

After that brief conference with his manager, Brooks steps back into the batter's box. Behind the plate, the Hurricanes catcher Danny McCormick signals for a pitch outside. Freeman tosses the ball wide of the plate. But Brooks reaches over and swings at it. What's going on here? Here comes the second pitch. Brooks reaches out and swings at this one as well. Amazing! Two strikes on pitches that are more than a foot outside the strike zone!

On the mound, Freeman looks angry. He takes the sign from his catcher and throws the ball even wider . . . too wide! The ball gets past McCormick! McGreevey races down to third on the wild pitch! The crowd loves it! Brooks tricked the pitcher into throwing the ball away!

Freeman fires his next pitch right down the center of the plate. Brooks gets under it and lifts a fly ball to deep rightfield. McGreevey tags up and races home ahead of the throw! The Comets close the gap, trailing now by a score of 4–2. MacKenzie and Lawrence follow with a walk and a single. Braxton hits a double into the rightfield corner that scores both men, tying the game at 4–4.

In the eighth, the Hurricanes bring in their stopper, Dave Cochran. The Comets leftfielder Aaron Parker gets hold of a Cochran fastball and hits it into the leftfield seats. Columbus leads, 5–4.

But the Hurricanes haven't surrendered by any means. Here in the ninth, they have staged a rally of their own. Pinch hitter Ned Cypher beat out an infield hit and then stole second. Wilson struck out, but Horka advanced Cypher to third on a bloop single to right.

That puts men at the corners with one out. And Ted Hartman is coming to bat. Braxton will have to be careful about how he pitches this .315 hitter. Hartman has hit 24 home runs this season. I'm sure he wouldn't mind another one right about now. The Comets are going to have to decide whether to play the outfield deep or to bring it in, in case they have a play at the plate.

If I have my outfielders play deep, nothing should get over their heads for extra bases. But they may be too far from the plate to have a real chance to throw a runner out trying to score. If I play them in, they have a better shot at catching little bloopers. But we could get burned on a ball that goes all the way back to the warning track in front of the outfield wall, particularly in the power alleys in right-center and left-centerfield. They don't pay me enough. . . .

▲ *To bring the outfield in, turn to page 88.*

▲ *To keep the outfield deep, turn to page 82.*

The Comets keep their outfield deep for the big bat of Ted Hartman. They figure he'll be swinging for the fences. The Comets pitcher Braxton looks in to the plate, sets and fires. Hartman swings. He hits a high fly ball into shallow center. Centerfielder Brooks is charging in, but he won't get there in time. Cypher scores from third and we're all tied up, 5–5! I'll bet the Comets manager is kicking himself for placing his outfielders so far back.

Braxton works his way out of the rest of the inning. That brings us to the Comets half of the ninth inning with the score even at 5–5. Against new reliever Lefty Merryman, Hatcher and McGreevey make two quick outs, each one popping out to the infield. But Brooks reaches first on a bad-hop single. MacKenzie moves him along with a hit just over the glove of the leaping first baseman.

Web Lawrence is due up. Lawrence's bat has been quiet all afternoon. He is struggling with a .260 average. This might be a good time to go to the bench and find a hotter hitter.

I know what everyone is thinking. Lawrence is in a slump. He hasn't hit the ball out of the infield since July. If we can push one run over here, we will win this thing. I've got Murphy

and Olson on the bench. I really ought to go with one of them.

But Lawrence looks hungry. He knows that he is overdue for a hit. Maybe he'll come through. A slump has to break sometime. Now?

▲ *To keep the batter in, turn to page 84.*

▲ *To put in a pinch hitter, turn to page 85.*

Well, I've got to say I'm surprised. With two out and two on, the Comets have elected to let Web Lawrence take his swings. The slumping rightfielder steps in against Merryman. The crowd has become awfully quiet.

Merryman throws two quick strikes to Lawrence. The bat never even left Web's shoulder. Lawrence steps out of the box and looks at the third base coach, Andy Kelley. Even from where I'm sitting, I can tell what the coach is saying. "Hit the ball."

Lawrence steps back in. Merryman looks in for the sign, then checks both of the runners. He kicks and fires . . . . Lawrence swings. It's a fly ball into shallow leftfield. Horka is backing up on the ball and Wilson is charging in on it. Wilson smashes into Horka just as the ball arrives. The two players fall to the grass . . . and so does the ball! Brooks is running on the play. He scores! Web Lawrence has knocked in the winning run! What a time to end a hitless string. The Comets are in the playoffs! What a fantastic game. What a fantastic *season!*

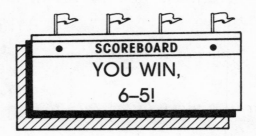

SCOREBOARD

YOU WIN,
6–5!

84

The Comets are going to pull Lawrence from the game, and send in the switch-hitting Ted Murphy to bat. Murphy is batting .307 and has hit 15 home runs. He has hit Merryman's pitching well in the past. The Comets have certainly turned up the heat on the Hurricanes.

But wait a minute! The Hurricanes have decided to give Murphy an intentional walk rather than pitch to him. That will load the bases. The Hurricanes want a play at every bag. They are also forcing the hand of the Comets manager, who must now decide what to do. His pitcher, Braxton, is due up, but nobody expects to see him bat.

I suspected they might pitch around Murphy. That only leaves me with Olson on the bench to pinch hit. Stan only bats from the left side and this Merryman is a hard-throwing left-hander. Well, I *do* have my secret weapon. I wonder if this is the time to try it out.

▲ *To put Olson in to pinch hit, turn to page 86.*

▲ *To put in your secret weapon, turn to page 87.*

The Comets send Stan Olson up to the plate. Olson stands in against the Hurricanes pitcher Merryman for the first time all season. He fouls off the first two pitches, then sends a tapper to third base. Rivera fields it cleanly and fires the ball to the plate. McCormick takes the throw and steps on the plate, ahead of the sliding Bo Brooks. What a rotten way to end a rally. So we move on to extra innings.

We're here in the top of the 12th inning with the score still tied at five apiece. Marty Braxton seems to be tiring. A fantastic play by Balzano robs Eubie Greene of a base hit. But then Braxton loses Gearhardt on an outside pitch and walks him. Carlos Rivera steps up and laces a double into the rightfield corner. McCormick follows Rivera with a single to deep center, scoring both Gearhardt and Rivera.

The Comets fail to produce in the bottom of the 12th. A tough loss for the home team. A long, long game at the end of a long, long season.

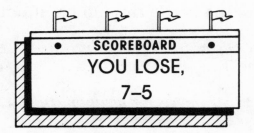

SCOREBOARD
YOU LOSE,
7–5

Well, will you look at that. The *manager* is pinch hitting! That's right, with the backup third baseman on the disabled list, there was room for one more player on the Comets roster. It never occurred to anyone that the team's manager would fill the slot. But here he is, stepping up to the plate: Mr. Wizard himself!

The Hurricanes pitcher Lefty Merryman throws every pitch he knows. The manager fouls off a couple and lays back on the rest. The count runs to three balls and two strikes. The runners will be going on the pitch. The entire season hangs on this pitch. Here comes the pitch. . . .

He bunts! The Comets manager lays down a perfect bunt along the first base line. By the time Cochran charges off the mound and picks up the ball, Brooks has crossed the plate and the manager has touched first. THE COMETS WIN! A pinch-hit bunt by the manager and the unbelievable Columbus Comets are rocketing off to the playoffs! I've never seen anything like it. The crowd pours down onto the field. The fans have the manager up on their shoulders! They call him "Mr. Wizard," and now you know why. This one will go down in the history books!

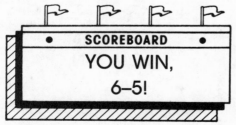

SCOREBOARD

YOU WIN,
6–5!

It looks like the Comets are going to gamble on this one. The manager has signaled to his outfield that he wants them to play up close. That means that all Hartman has to do is hit the ball over their heads and the game will be all tied up.

Comets pitcher Braxton will try to keep the ball low so that Hartman will hit it on the ground. Here comes the pitch . . . low. Hartman takes a golf swing and hits a high one-iron to leftfield. Flash Parker turns and takes off running at full speed. The ball is sailing back . . . back . . . . Flash digs hard, then looks over his shoulder and dives . . . . He's got it! A running, diving catch to rob the Hurricanes of the hit!

But wait. It looks like Cypher didn't tag up on the play. He dashed home! Now he's running back to third. Parker, on his feet again, fires the ball to Mac-Kenzie . . . in time! Double play! The Comets have won the game.

This one has been a real nail-biter, folks, but the Comets have pulled it off! On to the playoffs!

SCOREBOARD

YOU WIN,
5–4!